# CATS SET VI

# BRITISH SHORTHAIR CATS

Jill C. Wheeler
ABDO Publishing Company

## visit us at
## www.abdopublishing.com

Published by ABDO Publishing Company, PO Box 398166, Minneapolis, MN 55439.
Copyright © 2012 by Abdo Consulting Group, Inc. International copyrights reserved
in all countries. No part of this book may be reproduced in any form without written
permission from the publisher. The Checkerboard Library™ is a trademark and logo of
ABDO Publishing Company.

Printed in the United States of America, North Mankato, Minnesota.
102011
012012

PRINTED ON RECYCLED PAPER

Cover Photo: Photo by Helmi Flick
Interior Photos: AP Images pp. 11, 21; Photos by Helmi Flick pp. 5, 7, 9, 12, 13, 15, 19;
    Photo Researchers p. 17; Thinkstock pp. 11, 14–15

Editors: Megan M. Gunderson, BreAnn Rumsch
Art Direction: Neil Klinepier

### Library of Congress Cataloging-in-Publication Data

Wheeler, Jill C., 1964-
  British shorthair cats / Jill C. Wheeler.
     p. cm. -- (Cats)
  Includes index.
  ISBN 978-1-61783-239-0
  1. British shorthair cat--Juvenile literature.  I. Title.
  SF449.B74W44 2012
  636.8'2--dc23
                                                    2011026468

# CONTENTS

# LIONS, TIGERS, AND CATS

From house cats to lions, there are nearly 40 cat species. Large or small, all these cats have something in common. They belong to the family **Felidae**.

Researchers have traced the first members of the cat family back about 37 million years. The Egyptians were among the first to **domesticate** these animals. More than 3,500 years ago, they began using cats to control mice, rats, and other pests.

Today, people value domestic cats as companion animals. In US homes, there are more than 90 million pet cats. In fact, there are more pet cats than pet dogs!

Felines easily capture the hearts of their human companions. Cat lovers enjoy their personalities, ease of care, and ability to purr to show contentment. British shorthair cats have another winning quality. It is their special smile.

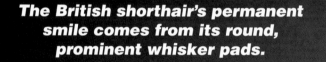

The British shorthair's permanent smile comes from its round, prominent whisker pads.

# BRITISH SHORTHAIR CATS

The British shorthair cat's permanent smile has made this very old **breed** famous! These well-known cats trace their history back to ancient Rome. The Romans brought their cats with them to Britain. There, the cats became important mouse catchers.

In the late 1800s, humans began refining the breed based on color and other qualities. In 1871, British shorthair cats appeared in the first formal cat show held in England.

Their popularity soared in the years that followed. Yet by the mid-1900s, the breed had lost favor and few remained. Thankfully, cat fanciers saved this historic breed from extinction.

British shorthairs, or Brits, remain fairly rare in the United States. In 1980, British shorthair cats were granted championship status in the **Cat Fanciers' Association (CFA)**.

*British shorthairs are among the oldest English cat breeds. They have long been admired for their strength and hunting skills.*

# QUALITIES

British shorthair cats are great house cats for families on the go. They are easy-going, non-destructive, low-energy pets. They do not need other animals for company. But, they have a good temperament for getting along with children, dogs, birds, and other cats.

Brits have a calm, quiet nature. They will curl up next to you on the couch to be petted. But, they are not the type of cat to curl up on a lap. And they do not like to be picked up and held.

Generally, Brits will determine the amount of attention they need. They like to be in the same room with people. Sometimes they will even follow their owners from room to room, watching everything.

*Brits are usually quiet, but they will meow sometimes.*

Brits are patient, intelligent animals, so animal trainers enjoy working with them. They also like playing with toys. They can even learn to play fetch!

# COAT AND COLOR

One of the British shorthair cat's many enjoyable features is its short, **dense** coat. Touching a Brit's coat is like rubbing your hands through a thick, luxurious carpet!

Brits can be a variety of solid colors. They are most known for blue. This is another name cat experts use to describe gray coats. Brits can also be white, black, red, cream, chocolate, or lavender. Some have **tabby** or tortoiseshell coats. Tortoiseshell coats feature red and black coloring.

This charming **breed** also has a wide range of eye colors. Copper, gold, hazel, green, blue green, and sapphire blue are all possible. Sometimes, a Brit's eyes are each a different color! All of these color options give Brits very striking eyes.

The **CFA** recognizes certain eye, nose, and paw pad colors for each coat color. Depending on coat color, a Brit's nose may be pink, black, brick red, blue, or old rose. Paw pads may be pink, black, brown, brick red, blue, or rose.

*A Brit's coat is more dense than any other cat breed's.*

# SIZE

Some cat **breeds** are lean and leggy like ballerinas. British shorthair cats are just the

opposite. They have been compared to football players! Cat breeders describe them as having a cobby, or stocky, build.

A Brit's muscular, stout body boasts a broad chest. This cat carries itself on short, thick legs and round paws. The Brit also has big, round, wide-set eyes and

*Brits have medium, rounded ears and round faces. People often compare them to teddy bears!*

12

bulging, round whisker pads. A large, rounded head and short, thick neck add to its stout appearance.

The Brit is one of the larger cat **breeds**. A full-grown male weighs about 9 to 17 pounds (4 to 8 kg). A female is slightly smaller, weighing 7 to 12 pounds (3 to 5.5 kg).

The Brit's tail is thick at the base with a rounded tip.

# CARE

British shorthairs are low-maintenance cats. In general, they are healthy. Yet like other cats, Brits should have annual checkups with a veterinarian. The veterinarian will provide **vaccines** and can **spay** or **neuter** cats that will not be **bred**. He or she will also check a Brit's teeth and gums.

Brits are completely comfortable being indoors and do not require time outside. Still, owners are

*British shorthairs should be kept indoors. There, owners should provide scratching posts so their cats can sharpen their claws.*

urged to play with their Brits.  Owners should provide a variety of toys to encourage exercise.

Although they have thick fur, Brits do not require a lot of grooming.  Their coats do not **mat** or tangle easily.  Usually, combing weekly with a metal comb is all that is needed.  This will remove loose hairs and dirt.  It is especially helpful when Brits **shed** in the spring and fall.

Exercise helps prevent obesity, which can be a problem for this breed.

# FEEDING

Cats are natural meat eaters, so their food should contain meat! This is included in high-quality dry foods. Moist and semimoist foods are also available. Owners should look for food labels that say "complete" and "balanced." And don't forget, Brits require a daily supply of fresh water.

Brits can have weight problems. No special food is required for healthy Brits. But you should prevent your cat from eating too much. Middle-aged cats are most likely to have weight issues. Therefore, feeding controlled portions twice a day is recommended.

**Obesity** can actually shorten a Brit's life span. If your Brit becomes obese, a low-calorie food and increased exercise can address this problem.

**Your veterinarian can recommend the healthiest diet based on your cat's age and physical condition.**

# KITTENS

As mothers, British shorthairs are loving and attentive. They can have up to three **litters** per year. Each litter usually contains four to five large, energetic kittens.

At first, the kittens are blind and deaf. But their eyes open in less than a week, and they can soon hear. By three weeks old, they begin to eat solid food. When they are 12 to 16 weeks old, Brit kittens are old enough to live away from their mother.

Brit owners should be sure their kittens have been tested to find out their blood type. While most cats have type A blood, many British shorthairs have the rare type B. This should be noted in the cat's medical records in case of an emergency.

British shorthairs mature slowly.  It can take five years
for them to reach their full size and weight!

# Buying a Kitten

British shorthairs make wonderful pets, but any pet is a great responsibility. Is a British shorthair's personality right for you and your family? If so, look for a reputable **breeder**.

There may be a long waiting list for these somewhat rare cats. So plan ahead. And remember, show-quality kittens are more expensive than pet-quality kittens.

When it is finally time to choose a kitten, make sure it is healthy! A Brit kitten should look strong, with good muscle tone. Its eyes and ears should be clean, and its nose should be cool and slightly moist.

A kitten should have started receiving **vaccines**, and it should be trained to use a **litter box**. Also, make sure the breeder has begun properly

*Brits will bond with the whole family, rather than just one owner.*

**socializing** it.  You will need to continue introducing your young, fluffy cat to everyday life and new people.

British shorthair cats are known for their energy and health.  With proper care and feeding, your cat will be a loving family member for 10 to 15 years or more.

# GLOSSARY

**breed** - a group of animals sharing the same ancestors and appearance.  A breeder is a person who raises animals.  Raising animals is often called breeding them.

**Cat Fanciers' Association (CFA)** - a group that sets the standards for judging all breeds of cats.

**dense** - thick or compact.

**domesticate** - to adapt something to life with humans.  Something domestic is tame, especially relating to animals.

**Felidae** (FEHL-uh-dee) - the scientific Latin name for the cat family.  Members of this family are called felids.  They include lions, tigers, leopards, jaguars, cougars, wildcats, lynx, cheetahs, and domestic cats.

**litter** - all of the kittens born at one time to a mother cat.

**litter box** - a box filled with cat litter, which is similar to sand.  Cats use litter boxes to bury their waste.

**mat** - to form into a tangled mass.

**neuter** (NOO-tuhr) - to remove a male animal's reproductive glands.

**obesity** - the condition of having too much body fat.

**shed** - to cast off hair, feathers, skin, or other coverings or parts by a natural process.

**socialize** - to adapt an animal to behaving properly around people or other animals in various settings.

**spay** - to remove a female animal's reproductive organs.

**tabby** - a coat pattern featuring stripes or splotches of a dark color on a lighter background. Individual hairs are banded with light and dark colors.

**vaccine** (vak-SEEN) - a shot given to prevent illness or disease.

# WEB SITES

To learn more about British shorthair cats, visit ABDO Publishing Company online. Web sites about British shorthair cats are featured on our Book Links page. These links are routinely monitored and updated to provide the most current information available.

**www.abdopublishing.com**

# INDEX

# A SERIES OF UNFORTUNATE EVENTS

## SUPPLEMENTARY MATERIALS

# Lemony Snicket

# THE LUMP OF COAL

*Art by* Brett Helquist

HARPERCOLLINS PUBLISHERS

The Lump
of Coal
Text copyright
© 2008 by
Lemony Snicket
Illustrations copyright
© 2008 by Brett Helquist

Printed in the U.S.A.

Library of Congress Cataloging-in-Publication Data
Snicket, Lemony.
The lump of coal / by Lemony Snicket ; art by Brett Helquist. —
1st ed.
p. cm.
Summary: A lump of coal that wants to be an artist, but would settle for making decorative marks on a
piece of grilled meat, rolls out of a forgotten bag of charcoal one winter and rolls through town seeking a
miracle.
ISBN 978-0-06-157428-3 (trade bdg.) — ISBN 978-0-06-157425-2 (lib. bdg.)
[1. Coal—Fiction. 2. Miracles—Fiction. 3. Christmas—Fiction.] I. Helquist, Brett, ill. II. Title.
PZ7.S6795Lum 2008                                                                 2007041931
[Fic]—dc22                                                                              CIP
                                                                                            AC

Book design by
Alison Donalty
1 3 5 7 9 10 8 6 4 2
❖ First Edition

# THE LUMP OF COAL

The holiday season is a time for storytelling, and whether you are hearing the story of a candelabra staying lit for more than a week, or a baby born in a barn without proper medical supervision, these stories often feature miracles. Miracles are like pimples, because once you start looking for them you find more than you ever dreamed you'd see, and this holiday story features any number of miracles, depending on your point of view.

The story begins with a lump of coal, who for the sake of argument could think, talk, and move itself around. Like many people who dress in black, the lump of coal was interested in becoming an artist. The lump of coal dreamed of a miracle—that one day it would get to draw rough, black lines on a canvas or, more likely, on a breast of chicken or salmon filet by participating in a barbeque.

But barbeques, sadly, are for summer, and this is a holiday story and so takes place in the dead of winter, when the air is gray and wet shoes line up in the hallways, shivering and crying tears of sleet. It is difficult to find a barbeque in the winter, although it is easy to find small animals scurrying through backyards and tipping things over such as abandoned snow-covered lawn chairs, frozen birdbaths, and forgotten bags of charcoal, and this is how the small, flammable hero of our story found itself tumbling out into the world.

"This isn't the miracle I was hoping for," said the lump of coal, "but perhaps if I roll around a bit I can find something interesting."

The lump of coal rolled out of the backyard, taking care to avoid the inevitable puddles of winter, and soon found itself in the center of town. You would think that the center of town would be bustling during the holiday season, but most shoppers were bustling around at the mall several miles away, so there was plenty of room on the sidewalk for the lump of coal.

It window-shopped for a while, and then to its delight the lump of coal found itself outside an art gallery. In the window were several paintings that looked like someone had taken a dark, crumbly substance and smeared it all over a piece of paper.

"I can't believe it!" cried the lump of coal. "Here is an art gallery that displays art by lumps of coal! It's a miracle!"

When the lump of coal rolled inside, however, it discovered that the art gallery was not a miracle after all. "We do not represent artists such as yourself," said the gallery owner after the lump of coal had introduced itself. The gallery owner had a long, oily mustache and a strange accent that the lump of coal suspected was fake. "We have a wide selection of works by human beings that suits us just fine. Please go away, and don't leave smudges on my artistic floor."

Disappointed, the lump of coal rolled outside. "That wasn't the artistic opportunity I was hoping for," it said to itself. "But if I roll around a bit more, perhaps I can find something interesting."

The lump of coal rolled farther down the block, and stopped in front of a building where powerful smells were wafting, a phrase which here means "coming from nearby, even though the door was closed." A sign on the building informed passersby

that the building was named MR. WONG'S
KOREAN BARBEQUE PALACE & SECRETARIAL
SCHOOL, which made the lump of coal gasp in
delight, because I forgot to tell you that for the
sake of argument the lump of coal could read.

"It's a miracle!" cried the lump of coal, and certainly there was every reason to believe this was so. A Korean restaurant is an excellent opportunity to enjoy an indoor barbeque—in fact, many such establishments have small barbeque pits installed in the tables, so you can do the barbequing yourself. I have spent many pleasant evenings in Korean restaurants, taking shelter from the winter cold, warming myself by the barbeque pit at my table, and enjoying the smell of the toasted rice tea, eggplant salad, and pickled cabbage served alongside the roasted meats and vegetables.

When the lump of coal rolled inside, however, it discovered that Mr. Wong's Korean Barbeque Palace and Secretarial School was not a miracle after all. The air was filled with the smell of oregano, which is not a Korean spice, and the owner was wearing a pair of very ugly earrings and a rude scowl on her face. "I don't need any coal," she said. "I get all my coal from a Korean restaurant supply factory. Everything in this restaurant has to be one hundred percent Korean."

"But Wong isn't even a Korean name," the lump of coal said. "And judging by the smell, I don't think you're using proper Korean spices."

"Please go away," said the restaurant owner, "and don't leave smudges on my Korean floor."

The lump of coal did what it was told, and began to grow very despondent, a word which here means "certain that a miracle would not occur after all." "Perhaps miracles only happen to human beings," it said, "or maybe miracles are only as genuine as Mr. Wong's Korean Barbeque Palace and Secretarial School. Perhaps I should just bury myself and become a diamond after thousands of years of intense pressure."

"Santa Claus!" cried the lump of coal. "It's a miracle!"

"I'm not a miracle," said Santa Claus, "and I'm not really Santa Claus. I'm an employee of the drugstore, dressed up and giving out coupons. The real Santa Claus is at the mall."

"Do you have any use for me?" asked the lump of coal. "I'm an artist at heart, but I'm very helpful when cooking meat."

Santa Claus sighed. "Well," he said, "my stepson is a very disobedient boy named Jasper. His mother used to say he had an artistic temperament, but I think he's a brat. You're just the thing to put in his stocking as punishment."

Just when the lump of coal was ready to return to its bag in the backyard, however, it ran into someone I'm sure I don't have to introduce. He was an overweight man with a long, white beard, dressed in a very bright red suit.

"I guess that's better than nothing," the lump of coal said, and when Santa Claus put him in Jasper's stocking, the lump of coal found that being in a cozy sock was, in fact, better than nothing. And when Jasper found the lump of coal, things became even better than better than nothing.

"A lump of coal!" Jasper cried. "I've been wanting to create some abstract art featuring rough, black lines!"

"I'd be happy to be of assistance," said the lump of coal.

"Egad!" cried Jasper. "You can talk! It's a miracle!"

It was a miracle, although the miracles didn't stop there.

Jasper and the lump of coal collaborated on a number of remarkable objets d'art, which the art gallery sold for an enormous fortune. That was a miracle.

Jasper and the lump of coal used this fortune to visit Korea, where they had always wanted to go, and when they came back they bought the restaurant and turned it into a proper place, known as Yi Sang's Korean Barbeque Palace and Secretarial School, after the famous Korean poet who was unfairly imprisoned for crimes he did not commit. That was a miracle too. In the daytime the two friends cooked genuine Korean food, and in the evenings they produced works of abstract art, and they never saw Santa Claus again, although they heard he had been fired from the drugstore for making fun of someone who was buying a certain ointment.

All these things are miracles. It is a miracle if you can find true friends, and it is a miracle if you have enough food to eat, and it is a miracle if you get to spend your days and evenings doing whatever it is you like to do, and the holiday season—like all the other seasons—is a good time not only to tell stories of miracles, but to think about the miracles in your own life, and to be grateful for them, and that's the end of this particular story.